The Futures & Options Trading Cheat Code

Mantras that will always protect you no matter what happens

JK Bull

Futures Options

Call Put

Time to steal from the **Operators** in their own game

Publishing Mongers

First Published in **August 2024**

ISBN: 978-93-6356-727-6

PUBLISHING MONGERS

+91 9311101365

Distributed by: Watergies

Preface

How to earn from Futures and Options without falling in traps laid by the operator.

Foreword

This book is a way to navigate everyone that is out to get you. If you stick to what the author tells you, you will always be protected. You will navigate all the traps and understand what it means to play the market.

Acknowledgments

A heartfelt thanks to the publishing team for everything you have done for The Futures and Options Trading Cheat Code.

About the author

I could be someone who is speaking from experience, or I am someone who has learnt from the best, but I might be someone who is involved with the operators, and is somewhat tired of how they play you. I cannot say any more than that. Understanding the game is upto you. Take it or leave it.

Dedication

This one is still dedicated to everyone who has lost even a single cent in the market.

Introduction

You are just a player in an ocean of money and if you know how to fill up the bucket, you can create a mini ocean for yourself. You do not control the market, but you can ride the market for a hefty profit while capping your loss and making the time play for your team. Stick to these Mantras in the market, and you will never fall for another trap. Think of a market where you can gain everything, but in the worst case scenario not lose it all. Give it a try, and you will never look elsewhere. It is time you know The Futures and Options Trading Cheat Code

Prologue

Time always wins. There is nothing more powerful in the world, and you think you can win against time ?

Mantra no 1

Dumb Money

Dumb money, that is what the institutions call you. Are you dumb ? Do you think you can control the market ? You cannot. The bulls and bears are fighting with millions and billions in their war chest. All you can do is win while they fight. When two cats fight, it is the monkey that wins the prize. Comparing to the capital you are playing with, embrace the monkey.

Mantra no 2

Don't mess around with Time

Time always wins. There is nothing more powerful in the world, and you think you can win against time ? Theta decay is always going to get you. The choice is yours though, you can make it your friend, or you can fight against it. You might win a few battles, but time will always win the war.

Mantra no 3

Buy ?

Never buy. Let's say you are sure of the market to go up to a target and you buy a call. What if the market fights back, and it spends a few days before reaching your target. The target will be achieved, but you won't make a penny on it. Again, make time your friend.

Mantra no 4

Sell ?

Always imagine a nuclear bomb. What if a country fires a nuclear bomb, maybe in a third world country. The market is going to crash like never before and what if you had sold put, you are bound to be bankrupt the next morning.

Mantra no 5

Hedge

You need to sell and buy. If your target is market rising, sell a put, and buy a lower put. Time will work for you, and so will the market. You won't lose even a single cent if the market goes in your favour.

Mantra no 6

Bound to Screw up

Would you want to lose it all on one trade ? Are you ready to do that ? I hope not. When you are hedged, you know your maximum loss. You can strategise for unlimited profit, but your loss is fixed. How much do you want to risk on one trade, it is up to you and time will work for you. The longer you stay, the more you earn whereas if you buy, the longer you stay, the lesser you earn.

Mantra no 7

Holding Power

When you are buying, your holding power has it's limit. You can keep on buying for your average, but it won't always work out, because the decay plus unfavourable market conditions is going to eat you up. Believe it or not, we are sure of the market's momentum in a particular direction, but the market might not always be ready to head there just yet. When you sell, you never need to average out, because time will help you get there.

Mantra no 8

Don't go All in

It sounds amazing to hear or say all in, but this is not a gamble. You need to trade with percentages. There are various strategies where your loss is capped, use it in your favour. Always remember the nuclear bomb scenario, and think what if. If you are protected or hedged, you know that is the maximum you can lose on a trade even if all hell breaks loose.

Mantra no 9

Firefight

Never fight with the market in derivatives. While you are most definitely bound to win in stocks, you are most likely going to lose in derivatives. You take a trade, and you let it work its magic. Even if a day before the expiry, you are not in a favourable position, you will be better off at expiry. The market does it wonders, and theta decay helps you get there. Don't overplay with something you know is going to disappear on a particular date.

Mantra no 10

Maintain your Target

Once you are in a trade, just hope and pray that it hits where you want it to hit. As soon as you enter a trade, your job is done. Let the market work it's magic and let you achieve your target. Always go for range targets.

Mantra no 11

Maintain a Range

Let's say you are expecting the market to go up a hundred points. The market has been bullish and you are counting on the momentum. Strategise the range to the existing position that covers your hundred points upside, but it also protects your hundred points downside. Long call is a classic example where it can cover your upside as much as you want it to, and protects you on the downside too.

Mantra no 12

Patience

While buying involves an aggressive approach, selling and hedging will need you to be patient. As soon as you get in a favourable trade, you will start going green pretty soon. The hardest part is waiting for the green to increase, because it will increase every second and that depends on you, how much you want to wait on and wait for.

Mantra no 13

Know when to Exit

Let's assume you are covered for five hundred points upside, and five hundred points downside. You need to exit at four fifty points because you don't know when the market is going to get out of your range. But, if you have an extra week in between, then you can let the market play its magic. You need to evaluate how many trading sessions you have till expiry and how certain are you of the market getting in your range.

Mantra no 14

Avoid playing with Fire

You will earn maximum for an expiry in the future, but you will earn the quickest with a current expiry. You need to ask yourself what is the priority, with a current expiry, you will get a smaller range, but with a far expiry, you will get better profits along with a bigger range. Although, the time value of money cannot be ignored. So, decide yourself because the current expiry does not give you room for error.

Mantra no 15

Expect the Unexpected

Why does anyone make a loss ? Because they did not expect that coming. You need to expect it, and be prepared for it just in case. You are in the game and everyone is playing it. Be prepared to lose a battle to win the war.

Mantra no 16

Capital does not Matter

Play with percentages and you will keep growing. Multiple trades are unlikely to help you in winning with derivatives. Target growing with a percentage, and there will be no turning back.

Mantra no 17

Mix it Up

You should try to mix up your short trades with long trades if you can afford it. Let's assume a long trade is getting you a six to twenty percent return in a month. Now, a month is a long time, and a lot can change. Your loss is capped in your long trade, and even if things go wrong in a week, you have three more weeks for them to go right. Until then target a one percent return daily where you sell a hedged position and don't wait for expiry. You just sell, take your theta decay and exit with flying colours. It might feel scary in the beginning, but this is going to be a piece of cake once you get the hang of it.

Mantra no 18

Use current OI for next Expiry

Look at the Open Interest data for today's expiry, and then when you are confident about the enormous position of writers at a particular spot price, sell your hedged position for the next expiry and exit the same at end of session today. Just take up all that decay, and if things go wrong, you have an extra week to get there.

Mantra no 19

Across Expiries

Let's assume you are selling a particular call for the next expiry, but you are getting the hedged position in current expiry for pennies. Sell the next week expiry, and buy the current expiry. If things go in your direction, you get your prize. But, if things screw up. You sell your profitable current expiry lot and adjust your sell in the next week. This way you make a profit on your hedge, and play again with the sell.

Mantra no 20

Experimentation

You need to experiment your strategies. There are a lot of them and find out the ones you are most comfortable with. All of them are designed to help you become profitable, but all of them come with their pros and cons. Find the one that works best in your favour, and know when to exit.

Mantra no 21

Never stick to One

If one strategy was working for you until now, it is not necessary it will keep working. The market is a dynamic environment, and you need to keep evolving with it. Sometime it is bullish, sometimes it is bearish, sometimes it is just range bound. You need to think of these factors before making your strategy. Most strategies will cover either side, but not all will.

Mantra no 22

Fear

Fear is a good thing when it comes to derivatives. It makes you you careful. Always imagine what if it does not work out. Imagine your worst case scenario. Can you survive the outcome ? Will you able to trade again if this trade does not work out ? Think about it before you move forward, and the market is going to scare you constantly. Adapt to it.

Mantra no 23

Less is More

Your goal is to not lose. You can earn more, you can earn less, but try to never lose. With derivatives, you are bound to lose sometime, but not let that loss be big enough that it takes away whatever you have earned.

Mantra no 24

Capital Dip

First and foremost, protect your capital. If you learn how to protect your capital and move forward, you are never going to look back. Ensure that there is never a capital dip. Because if you lose 90 out of hundred, that is 90 percent. But to recover that 90, you need to earn 900 percent.

Mantra no 25

Goal

You need to have a goal in mind. You need to know that by expiry, your market should be here. If it is getting there, that is the best. But what if it gets there early. What will you do ? You need to have an outer range of that target, that is the point where you exit, with just a little green. A little green is better than red.

Mantra no 26

Don't listen to Predictions

It is your money, and you need to know what is right for it. If the person predicting it was so sure, they would be investing themselves, rather than predicting for others. There is no harm in listening, but don't let it influence your decision.

Mantra no 27

No to Economies of Scale

If you are in a stock, making multiple entries helps you because it never expires. But when it comes to derivatives, your money can go zero, so once you are in, just wait and watch. Play on something you can handle, and the market will reward you accordingly.

Mantra no 28

Future

If you are buying futures instead of options, it will work in your favour because decay won't eat you up. You need to hedge your futures with a put too, but that put is going to decay with time. So, if you are confident of a bullish future that beats your put premium, stay indefinitely. If not, buy, earn and exit as soon as you can.

Mantra no 29

The Good, the Bad and the Ugly

There will be good days, and there will be bad days. No matter how careful you are, there will be both. You need to balance them in order to succeed. Don’t let either of them influence your decisions, especially in the Ugly ones. Ugly ones are those where all you have is regret. A classic example is where you exit in red, because you have no hope of green and the moment you exit the market, the market reverses. That is the ugliest. Remain calm on that day and don’t trade. Sleep on it.

Mantra no 30

You are Alone

Once you are in the market, you are all alone and there is no one who can help you. As soon as you make a trade, all the decisions that you take are your responsibility and no one can help you win or make you lose. What you do from that moment forward, that is all on you.

Mantra no 31

Bull or Bear

Don't be succumbed to either side. Think of all the possibilities and evaluate the time you have to get there, and you are going to win it all.

Mantra no 32

Regret

You will always have regret. It might be that you exited early, it might be that you bought lesser quantity than you could. As long as you are exiting in green, have no regrets because you have more than you had yesterday.

Mantra no 33

Decision

You have to decide when you want to enter and when you want to exit. No one can help you with that. In the live market, you decide what lives and what dies. You are bound to make wrong decisions, don't worry, that is part of the process. That is how you will learn and you will perfect it.

Mantra no 34

Consider the Game

You have to know what is the most probable rise or fall, and where you will stand when that happens. You can only predict it and work accordingly and most of the times the market will respect that. Plan accordingly and cap your losses if the market becomes volatile.

Mantra no 35

Naked

Naked selling is the most lucrative route in the market. But, always remember the nuclear bomb scenario. Can you survive that ? In a bearish market, naked call selling helps with a lot of the factors, but where there is a fall, there is a place to rise. Whereas, in a bullish market, the top is an uncharted territory, and there is no stopping it. So, don't do naked selling because it might be the most lucrative route, but it is also the easiest way to wipe off your capital in one go.

Mantra no 36

Never Panic

More often than not, the market will go against you. It might be temporary, or the market might be taking a direction. It does not matter, just evaluate how many days you have and is there even a slight possibility of that turning around in the number of days you have. If you have that margin, ride it until the end. You will see how many times the market rewards you.

Mantra no 37

Ignore the Charts

The charts are meant to make you lose money. Trust the Open Interest. If n number of contracts have been written off at a particular spot price, they know what is going to happen. Trust your peers, because most of them will be the ones that influence the market. No one is going to write off a contract and work in the opposite direction just to lose money. If the market goes against them, they will try to bring it back in range.

Mantra no 38

Decline in OI

Whenever you see Open Interest declining a few points above or below, know that something is going to happen soon. Again, those who write, they have their sway and before they make their move, they will exit their positions.

Mantra no 39

Risk Reward

Always evaluate the Risk and the Reward. You should have the time in your favour, you should have more profit potential than the loss cap and you should have a range to operate in.

Mantra no 40

Insurance

This is the most difficult level to obtain, but if you look closely, you are going to get it from time to time. Let's say you are in the best position and you are bound to book a profit. Now, if you are riding it till the end in green, buy an OTM put and an OTM call in your profit range if you get them for much lower than your profit. That ensures wherever the market goes, you will always remain green.

Mantra no 41

Diversify or Focus

Now this has to be on the basis of what works out for you. Whether you want to trade in multiple expiries altogether if you can handle it or do you want to focus on just one and ignore the others. Both the approaches are correct, but you have to be decide which one suits you more.

Mantra no 42

Composure

You have to remain calm. If the market has been giving you returns on being bullish for a week, there is soon going to be a correction or a profit booking. Anticipate that, prepare for that and hope the market continues your direction. But if it does not, you need to be prepared just in case.

Mantra no 43

When

For an option buyer, there is nothing more important than the when. They need to be aware of the days and the possible decay before the market hits their target. But with a seller, the only when that matters is how green are you and how many days are left. You decide when you want to enter and how much green do you want to leave with.

Mantra no 44

Beware of Influencers

Social media is full of influencers predicting the direction of the market. Don’t listen to them. If they were correct, they would not be doing influencing, but rather they would be minting money. Have your own approach, learn the basics and predict yourself. At the end, it is you who will win or lose and not them.

Mantra no 45

Know when to Back out

This works when you have spent some time in a trade which means you are in green. You need to set an upper predefined spot and a lower predefined spot, and know that you will not wait above or below this range even if you expect a reversal because the market moves in its own direction. Learn when to

Mantra no 46

Zero Sum

Trading Futures and Options is a zero sum game. If you are earning, that means someone else is losing. No one is stupid enough to deliberately lose. If they are losing, they are either hedged or they made a mistake. Always remember you are going against seasoned investors, and they will not fall for a trap you lay out, but they have enough experience to trap you. Avoid all these traps as much as you can. And if you get caught, fight for your survival.

Mantra no 47

Don't use Leverage

When you use leverage, you are putting your capital at risk as well as your portfolio or your borrowings. Play with what you have and if thing don't work out, lose a small percentage of what you have and if you gain, step by step you are going to have more than you could have ever leveraged.

Mantra no 48

Scalp

If you enter a contract and you are green instantly, exit. You can take another position and earn more there. What you have earned from your current position instantly, that is going to stay with you and no matter what happens in the market, no one is going to be able to take it away from you.

Mantra no 49

Take out your Capital

Take out your capital as soon as you can and play with your profits because one day, it might be today, tomorrow or a few months from now, you are going to take a wrong trade or the market becomes volatile. Whatever happens, your capital will always be secure and that gives a lot of comfort in a panicked situation. It will help you take your decisions more rationally and you will be able to navigate the market

Mantra no 50

Now or Never

Everyday is a good day to trade, but you might not always be comfortable with it. Evaluate whether you have a likely prediction of the market's direction and trade accordingly. Everyday you are right, you earn something every second, every minute, every hour, slowly and steadily, but the moment you go wrong, you lose money. So trade according to your comfort zone and focus on the winning while eliminating the risk.

Target

Write your target here

Your personal strategy
Your personal Mantra

Write it down
You will need it soon

Strategies to Never Lose

THE FUTURES & OPTIONS STRATEGY CHEAT CODE

Mantric Strategies that will always always protect you

Strategies to be smart so that the **Operators** cannot get you

JK BULL

Stock Market Cheat Code

THE STOCK MARKET TRADING CHEAT CODE

Mantras that will never let you lose even a single dime

Time to cheat the **Operators** at their own game

Publishing Mongers

JK BULL

www.ingramcontent.com/pod-product-compliance
Lightning Source LLC
Chambersburg PA
CBHW061221240926
51846CB00006B/1303
9789363567276